2021

Creative Rhymes

Edited By Byron Tobolik

First published in Great Britain in 2021 by:

Young Writers
Remus House
Coltsfoot Drive
Peterborough
PE2 9BF
Telephone: 01733 890066
Website: www.youngwriters.co.uk

Printed and bound in the UK by BookPrintingUK
Website: www.bookprintinguk.com
YB0476E

FOREWORD

Dear Reader,

Welcome to this book packed full of feathery, furry and scaly friends!

Young Writers' Poetry Safari competition was specifically designed for 5-7 year-olds as a fun introduction to poetry and as a way to think about the world of animals. They could write about pets, exotic animals, dinosaurs or even make up their own crazy creature! From this starting point, the poems could be as simple or as elaborate as the writer wanted, using imagination and descriptive language.

Given the young age of the entrants, we have tried to include as many poems as possible. Here at Young Writers we believe that seeing their work in print will inspire a love of reading and writing and give these young poets the confidence to develop their skills in the future. Poetry is a wonderful way to introduce young children to the idea of rhyme and rhythm and helps learning and development of communication, language and literacy skills.

These young poets have used their creative writing abilities, sentence structure skills, thoughtful vocabulary and most importantly, their imaginations, to make their poems and the animals within them come alive. I hope you enjoy reading them as much as we have.

CONTENTS

Marsh Green Primary School, Marsh Green

Holly Griffiths (7)	54
Vinson He (7)	55
Sienna Myers (7)	56
Jack Birtwistle (7)	57
Ruby-Jean Foster-Finlay (7)	58
Leon Hogan (6)	59
Grace Rollins (7)	60
Ava-Mae Rollins (7)	61
Julia Lubowiecka (7)	62
Logan Davidson (7)	63
Lily Hoang (6)	64
Sienna Pennington (7)	65
Kasey Leyland (7), Libby, Sofia Popovici (7), Lewis Adams (7) & Ella-Mae Browitt (7)	66
Keira O'Connell (7)	67
Anson He (5)	68
Ezmai-Rose Pilling (6), Teja (5) & James Cullen (6)	69
Gabriella Zefelde (5)	70
Lexi Jo Gallagher (7)	71
Scarlett Highton (6)	72
Grace Liptrot (6)	73
Evie-Mai Sedgwick (6)	74
Samuel Mikolajow (7)	75
Jake Ademola (5)	76
Lola Cottom (7)	77
Alfie Wilson (7)	78
Adam Koufa (7) & Lacey	79
Patricia Zalitie (7)	80
Eki Osasuwen (7)	81
Wahaj Asim (7)	82
Ziyad Younis (5)	83
Leo Bradley (6)	84
James Hughes (6)	85
Khloe O'Neil (7)	86
Victoria Hardman (6)	87
Alex Kudinov (6) & Charlie	88
Ellie Allison (6)	89
Paul Doherty (7)	90
Declan Charnock (5)	91
Preston-Lee Dover (6)	92
Charlie-Joe Towert (6)	93
Jasmine Busby (6)	94
Annie Wheatcroft (6)	95
Nicola Jubass (6)	96
Emily Caine (6)	97
Oliwier Szymanski (6)	98
Amelia Wojtaluk (6)	99
Kristian Longshaw (6)	100
Aiden Yates (6)	101
Kaitlin Musgrove (5)	102
Jack Walker (6)	103
Leo Peet (6)	104

Saint Pierre School, Leigh-On-Sea

Jayden Bamfo (7)	105
Cornelius Oberholzer (7)	106
Keidi Okpue (7)	107
Holly Rye (7)	108
Phoebe Norris (7)	109
Pendo Mbugua (6)	110
Esmé Bragard (6)	111
Molly Dumpleton (7)	112
Monty Millson (7)	113
Ethan-Sanders Tafadzwa Kanyepi (7)	114
Henry Brown (5)	115
Bella Hemmings (6)	116
Marley Wilson (7)	117
Sara Khan (6)	118
Emmeline Longhurst (6)	119
Rory Wainwright (6)	120
Jorey Kyei-Bamfo (5)	121
Leo Jarvis (6)	122
Nelly Cottage (6)	123
Theodore Hoad (6)	124
Sabrina Dearson (6)	125

St Joseph's Catholic Primary School, Upminster

Frank Garvey (6)	126
Millie Lavey (7)	127
Maria Rasskazova (7)	128
Darcy Davies (7)	129
Molly Tobin (6)	130
Penny Restarick (7)	131
Patrick Fuller (7)	132
Anastazja Strzelczyk (7)	133
Somto Iwu (6)	134
Hugo Willis (7)	135
Olive Etherington (7)	136
Arthur Hill (7)	137
Grey Harding (7)	138
Kitty Tyler (6)	139
Elsie Hosler (6)	140
Oliver Holmes (8)	141
Lily Garrett (6)	142
Sophia Jackson (7)	143
Alice Fletcher (6)	144
Nico Vannoli Rogacz (7)	145
Elizabeth Mahoney (7)	146
Ryan Arun (7)	147
Millie Allen (6)	148

St Joseph's Catholic School, Malmesbury

Jago Sandilands (6)	149
Lara (5)	150
Finn Stannard (5)	151
Jaz (5)	152
Florence Gray (5)	153
Josh Davison (6)	154
Victoria Mroszczyk (5)	155
Rosalie Andreou (5)	156
Ottilie Beswick (5)	157
Caleb Chapman (4)	158
Thomas Pilkington (5)	159

St Vincent's Catholic Primary School, Penketh

Olivia Connor (7)	160
Clemency Ryan-Stout (7)	161
Lottie Corbett (7)	162
William Chaplin (7)	163
Daisy-Mai Winsor (7)	164
Elise Vernon (7)	165
Macy Winn (7)	166
Lottie Dean (7)	167
Isabelle Hodgkin (7)	168
Aimee Moss (7)	169
Rageh Biviji (6)	170
Harris Weston (6)	171
Mia Hughes (6)	172
Joel Gawne-Sheridan (6)	173
Frankie Lloyd (7)	174
Jessica Croughan (5)	175
Libby Thompson (6)	176
Thea Halsall (5)	177
Shannon Albinson (6)	178
Maddie Lockwood (6)	179
Daniel Moore (5)	180
Oliver Graham (5)	181
Bonnie Fagan (6)	182
Ivy Harrison (5)	183

The Poems

Cheetah

It is as fast as a leopard.
Its teeth are as sharp as a knife.
It is yellow and brown.
It can pounce like a bunny.
It is as scary as a black panther.
It eats meat.
It has round ears.
It is a cheetah.

Iris Clarke (7)
Brighstone CE Aided Primary School, Brighstone

1

Guinea Pigs!

Guinea pigs smell like hay and carrots.
Guinea pigs look as cute as a teddy.
Guinea pigs sound like a door squeaking.
Guinea pigs feel as fluffy as a pom-pom.
Guinea pigs taste like carrots and grass.

Poppy Jones (7)
Brighstone CE Aided Primary School, Brighstone

All About Parrotfish

Parrotfish smell like salt from the deep sea.
Parrotfish look creepy.
Parrotfish sound like the river running.
Parrotfish feel as slimy as slime.
Parrotfish taste like blood, eyes, rock and coral.

Seren Forster (6)
Brighstone CE Aided Primary School, Brighstone

Monkeys

Monkeys smell like bananas.
Monkeys look cheeky like mice.
Monkeys sound like *ooo, ooo, aaa, aaa!*
Monkeys feel scruffy and hairy.
Monkeys taste like bananas.

Reuben Lacey (7)
Brighstone CE Aided Primary School, Brighstone

Horse

Horse smells like hay and is smelly.
Horse looks like fast clip-clopping.
Horse sounds like clip-clopping.
Horse tastes like old hay.
Horse feels soft and fluffy.

Poppy Luff (7)
Brighstone CE Aided Primary School, Brighstone

Black Panther

They are as fast as a cheetah.
As black as the night sky.
As fierce as a snow leopard.
Its teeth are as sharp as a snake's teeth.
It's a black panther.

Ila Bland (7)
Brighstone CE Aided Primary School, Brighstone

Cats!

Cats smell like rotten fish.
Cats look like little black panthers.
Cats sound like squeaky deer.
Cats feel like smooth silk.
Cats taste like raw meat.

Lucy Warvill (7)

Brighstone CE Aided Primary School, Brighstone

The Horse

Horses smell like flies.
Horses look like cute teddies.
Horses sound like clip-cloppy hooves.
Horses feel soft like a bunny.
Horses taste like flies!

Charlotte Rayner (7)
Brighstone CE Aided Primary School, Brighstone

Owl

It flies in the sky.
It lives in trees.
They can turn their heads around.
It has a sharp beak.
It has fire-coloured eyes.
They hoot at night.

Isobel Rayner (7)
Brighstone CE Aided Primary School, Brighstone

Mr Fox

It is as big as a dog.
It has a white tummy.
It lives on the Isle of Wight.
It has long ears.
It has long legs like a dog.
It is a fox.

Freddie Harrison (6)
Brighstone CE Aided Primary School, Brighstone

Dogs

Dogs smell like sweaty socks.
Dogs look like teddy bears.
Dogs bark like a car alarm.
Dogs feel as soft as a blanket.
Dogs taste like bacon.

Emily Dance (7)

Brighstone CE Aided Primary School, Brighstone

Dogs

Dogs smell like fish biscuits.
Dogs look like gorillas.
Dogs sound like a fire alarm.
Dogs feel soft like a pillow.
Dogs taste like a sofa.

Thomas Cambridge (7)
Brighstone CE Aided Primary School, Brighstone

Mr Lemur

It is as soft as a peach.
It is as good at climbing as a monkey.
It is as fast as people.
It has big spooky eyes.
It is black and white.

Christopher Hearn Morales (6)
Brighstone CE Aided Primary School, Brighstone

All About Koalas

K oalas climb trees
O n a branch
A re cuddly
L ikes eucalyptus leaves
A lways sleeping.

Toby Bacon (7)
Brighstone CE Aided Primary School, Brighstone

14

Monkeys

Monkeys look like human babies,
Leopard and crocodiles are their enemies.

Monkeys like to eat bananas,
They always wear pyjamas.
They are cheeky! They are funny!
They say, "Na, na, na, ne, na!"

They swing from tree to tree,
They always feel free.
They are so greedy with food,
Dora's monkey is called Boots.

They live in the jungle,
They are never single.
They are always having a mingle,
Sometimes their tails get in a tangle.

Roelan Rishan (7)
Gosberton Academy, Gosberton

Angus The Angry Ant

Angus was an angry ant,
Who often used to rave and rant.
He wouldn't work, he wouldn't play,
"What's wrong with him?" his friends would say.

One day at school, he lost the plot,
And missed his favourite break time slot.
He threw his pen and shook his head,
And turned a vivid shade of red.

"What's wrong?" his worried teacher asked,
"It's not like you can't do these tasks.
No one wants to see you cry,
All we ask is that you try."

"I try," moaned Angus in a huff,
"I just don't think it's good enough."
"Of course it is, if it's your best,"
Said teacher, "That's all we request."

"So it's okay to be behind the others,
Wow, I thought you'd mind
that I was slow and diligent,
And looking unintelligent."

"Oh Angus, please don't worry, mate,
Don't get yourself in such a state.
Just try your hardest every day,
And let your anger fade away."

Through hard work, Angus found a way,
To finish work on time each day.
He turned into a real grafter,
And loved his school work ever after!

Ross McClements (6)

Gosberton Academy, Gosberton

Unicorn

U nicorns are awesome, shooting rainbows from their horns

N ever lost in the woods, always home before dawn

I t eats colourful flowers, its body is a rainbow

C ones and ice cream are its favourite thing, even in the snow

O h, it is so beautiful, it is the national animal of Scotland

R eady to go to the beach, its favourite part is the sand

N ever forget, a unicorn is the most magical thing in the world.

Freya Newell (7)
Gosberton Academy, Gosberton

The Pig

There was a pig who lived on a farm,
He was pink and round and very, very calm.
He loved the sound of the old farm,
It had such a great charm.
The days flew by as he rolled in the mud,
He had an awesome time playing with his buds.
As the day came to an end,
He closed his eyes and said goodnight.

Austin George Clarke (7)
Gosberton Academy, Gosberton

Frozen Ice

Ice is cold, fire is hot,
This creature named Ice likes it a lot.
It likes the dark, but not the light,
That's why you only see it at night.
It goes in water for only ten minutes,
Any longer, you'd have to bin it.
Its feathers glow, its body shades,
That's just how it is made.

Ben Tamplin (5)
Gosberton Academy, Gosberton

The Singer Bear

The bear likes to sing all day long
And this is the bear's favourite song...
"Da de dum, let's all have fun,
Looking at the sky so very high,
We go to the park and play until it's dark.
Then the moon starts to rise,
So we go home and a whole new day
starts."

Jessica Parker (6)
Gosberton Academy, Gosberton

Shark Bite

I'm scary,
Not a fairy or hairy.
I'm fast,
Not slow or last.
I'm clever,
Not silly like a feather.
I swim,
I don't run in the sun.
I bite,
I don't slurp or burp.
I'm a shark
That lives in the dark.

Olly Mason (7)
Gosberton Academy, Gosberton

A Lion On The Prowl

A lion on the prowl,
A lion that can growl.
A lion with a mane,
But without a gold chain.
A lion that can purr,
With golden, fluffy fur.
A lion tiptoes on the land he owns,
A lion roams around the old bones.

Reuben Sandall (7)

Gosberton Academy, Gosberton

In The Clouds!

Candy Fun in the clouds,
Dancing near the sun,
Eating lots of bubblegum.
Jumping on the clouds with his friends,
Candy Fun's fun never ends.
At night, he sleeps on the clouds,
On his own, snoring loud.

Evelyn Crowson (7)
Gosberton Academy, Gosberton

The Octopus

O ctopus
C an change shape
T o squeeze through gaps
O nly under the sea
P rawns are their favourite food
U tterly long legs
S uckers help it move.

Wyn Skinner (5)
Gosberton Academy, Gosberton

Cheetahs

Cheetahs are fast.
Cheetahs eat meat.
They think on their feet.
They hide in the long grass.
In the world, there are 100,500 cheetahs.
Cheetahs bite throats to suffocate their prey.

Eliza Ginger-Davis (6)
Gosberton Academy, Gosberton

The Flamingo

A sea of pink feathers,
Standing on one foot,
Bobbing up and down,
Looking for fish,
Flying high in the sky,
Off to go to sleep.

Holly Smith (6)

Gosberton Academy, Gosberton

The Great Gorilla

G argantuan, black, strong gorilla slowly wandering

O nly one wise silverback in the troop

R ainforest south of the Sahara

I love gorillas because they are caring and powerful

L eaves are juicy, green and delicious for gorillas

L arge and intelligent, hairy and magnificent, protecting their family

A gorilla can walk on its knuckles.

Rosie-May Violet Steventon (7)

Hazel Leys Academy, Corby

The Great Gorilla

G argantuan, black, strong gorilla slowly wandering

O nly one wise silverback in the troop

R ainforest south of the Sahara

I love gorillas because they are powerful and caring

L eaves are juicy, green and delicious

L arge and intelligent, hairy and magnificent, protecting their family

A gorilla walks proudly on its knuckles.

Tiago Sousa (7), Edgar, Cameron Mcdonald (7), Emily (7), Layla-J (7), Mateusz (7), David Szewczyk (7) & Blake (7)

Hazel Leys Academy, Corby

The Great Gorilla

G igantic, black, strong gorilla wandering slowly

O nly one wise silverback in the troop

R ainforest south of the Sahara

I love gorillas because they are powerful and caring

L eaves are juicy, green and delicious

L arge and intelligent, hairy and magnificent at protecting their family

A gorilla walks proudly on its knuckles.

Deacon Jones (7)
Hazel Leys Academy, Corby

The Great Gorilla

G argantuan, black, strong gorilla slowly wandering

O nly one wise silverback in the troop

R ainforest south of the Sahara

I love gorillas because they are powerful and caring

L eaves are juicy, green and delicious

L arge and intelligent, hairy and magnificent, protecting

A gorilla walks proudly on its knuckles.

Lexie Walker (7)
Hazel Leys Academy, Corby

The Great Gorilla

G argantuan, black, strong gorilla slowly wandering

O nly one wise silverback in the troop

R ainforest south of the Sahara

I love gorillas because they are powerful and caring

L eaves are juicy, green and delicious

L arge and intelligent, hairy and magnificent

A gorilla walks proudly on its knuckles.

Lily Benko (7)
Hazel Leys Academy, Corby

The Great Gorilla

G argantuan, black, strong gorilla slowly wandering

O nly one wise silverback in the troop

R ainforest south of the Sahara

I love gorillas because they are wise

L eaves are juicy, green and delicious

L arge and smart, hairy and magnificent, they protect their family

A gorilla walks on its knuckles.

Bailie Pyper (6)

Hazel Leys Academy, Corby

The Great Gorilla

G argantuan, black, strong gorilla slowly wandering

O nly one silverback

R ainforest south of the Sahara

I love gorillas because they are powerful and caring

L eaves are juicy, green and delicious

L arge and intelligent, hairy and magnificent

A gorilla walks proudly on its knuckles.

George Kobbey (7)
Hazel Leys Academy, Corby

The Great Gorilla

G argantuan, black, strong gorilla slowly wandering

O nly one wise silverback in the troop

R ainforest south of the Sahara

I love gorillas because they are powerful

L eaves are juicy and delicious

L arge and magnificent

A gorilla walks on its knuckles.

Landon Boyd (7)
Hazel Leys Academy, Corby

The Quick Cheetah

C heetahs are speedy with loud roars
H abitat is found on a safari
E xtremely rapid and fast
E nergetic animals
T hey are extremely endangered
A re very spotty
H ungry because the more running they do,
   the more hungry and sleepy they get.

Hayden Hanson (6)
Hazel Leys Academy, Corby

What Lives In A Jungle?

I am furry.
I have four legs.
I am black.
I am big and strong.
I hunt for meat.
I live in the jungle.
I have best friends.
I have a cub.
I love swimming.
I am a panther!

Jay-Oliver Singh (6)
Hazel Leys Academy, Corby

What Am I?

I have wings but I am not a bird.
I have six legs but I am not an ant.
I love nectar but I am not a bee.
I lay eggs but I am not a hen.
I am a butterfly!

Jonathan Wisnicki (6)

Hazel Leys Academy, Corby

Elephants

Elephants like to walk.
Elephants live in Africa.
Elephants eat fruit.
Elephants are grey.
Elephants are big and healthy.
Elephants like family.

Niyah-Marni Chuplis (6)

Hazel Leys Academy, Corby

What Am I?

I am cheeky.
I am black.
I am fluffy.
I am big.
I eat bananas.
I live in a jungle.
I like to swing in the trees.
I am a gorilla!

Bogdans Paradniks (6)
Hazel Leys Academy, Corby

What Am I?

I am brown.
I sleep in the grass.
I lie in the jungle.
I look like a stick.
I wish I could fly.
I have six legs.
I am a stick insect!

Giulia Cosma (6)
Hazel Leys Academy, Corby

What Am I?

I like to play with my owner.
I like tickles on my belly.
I like to eat meat.
I like walks to the field.
What am I?
I am a dog!

Frankie Widdowson (6)
Hazel Leys Academy, Corby

Foxes

Foxes are small and orange.
Foxes eat chickens.
Foxes live in dens.
Foxes hunt.
Foxes are clever.
Foxes are scared of humans.

Krzysztof Bugajski (6)

Hazel Leys Academy, Corby

What Am I?

I am brown and soft.
I am small.
I have four legs.
I like to sleep.
I love to play.
I am naughty.
I am a cat!

Naomi Thar (6)
Hazel Leys Academy, Corby

Guess What He Is!

He eats lots of chickens.
He digs fast.
He jumps high.
He runs very fast.
He has fluffy, orange fur.
He is a fox!

Antoni Sowinski (6)
Hazel Leys Academy, Corby

My Tiger

My tiger eats meat.
My tiger walks in the jungle.
My tiger has stripes.
My tiger likes to run.
My tiger is happy.

Filip Brzezinski (5)
Hazel Leys Academy, Corby

Elephants

I am cute and beautiful.
Elephants eat plants and fruit.
I am an African elephant.
Elephants like to walk around.

Nella Tancosova (6)
Hazel Leys Academy, Corby

What Am I?

I like to play.
I have stripes all over me.
I love my people.
I wish I was pink and purple.
I am a cat.

Marianna Jegorova (6)
Hazel Leys Academy, Corby

What Am I?

I am nice and cute.
I eat meat.
I am little.
I live at home.
I like to play.
I am a sausage dog!

Olivia McHugh (5)
Hazel Leys Academy, Corby

Gorillas

Gorillas like to eat plants.
Gorillas are tall and big.
Gorillas are black.
Gorillas live in Africa.

Antonia Ignat (6)
Hazel Leys Academy, Corby

Who Is He?

He likes to walk.
He hunts mice.
He plays with a ball.
He likes to sleep.
He is a cat!

Dragan Zelnik (5)
Hazel Leys Academy, Corby

All About Cats

I am a cat.
I sit on a mat.
I chase a rat.
I wear a hat.
And that is that!

Dolcie Pettey (6)

Hazel Leys Academy, Corby

What Am I?

I eat bananas.
I climb.
I am cheeky.
I have a long tail.
I am a monkey.

Doruk Yayla (6)

Hazel Leys Academy, Corby

The Mysterious Animal

It has a big grey trunk and a strong, soft body like a ruler.
It has a firm, silky body like a mattress.
It has a big cute head like the leaves on trees.
It has grey skin like a gorilla.
It has huge silky ears like a flag blowing in the wind.
It has strong, long, thick legs like a chair.
It has pointy white tusks like a rhino's horns.
It has a small, tiny brain like a cute little bird.
It has cute stomping feet like a running zebra.
It has fabulous shins like a soft monkey.
What is it?

Answer: *An elephant.*

Holly Griffiths (7)
Marsh Green Primary School, Marsh Green

The One Animal

It has a round yellow belly like a toy car that is yellow.
It has a skinny tail like an elephant.
It has black hooves like a zebra.
It has a nose like a human.
It has squashed legs like an ostrich.
It has a long neck like a school fence.
It has ears like a cat's.
It has a herbivore mouth that is only eating plants.
It has a head like a zebra.
It has antennae like a butterfly.
It has pupils in its eyes like a tiger.
It has a bottom like a lion.
What is it?

Answer: A giraffe.

Vinson He (7)
Marsh Green Primary School, Marsh Green

The Lovely Zoo Of Secrets

It has brown, strong legs like a horse.
It has small, beady eyes like a fly.
It is grey and white like a bull.
It has dark brown skin like a bear.
It has tiny ears like a monkey.
It is small and cute like a turtle.
It is strong like a gorilla.
It lives in Africa and Canada like elephants.
It eats creamy green avocado.
It runs around all day like a bull.
It relaxes all day like a tiger.
It has small, tiny ears like a cat.
It has a tiny, wet, soggy nose like a cat and a dog.
What is it?

Sienna Myers (7)
Marsh Green Primary School, Marsh Green

The Magical Zoo

It has long shiny legs like a tree.
It has huge sharp teeth like a lion.
It has a wet white nose like a dog in a pool.
It has beady eyes like a ladybug.
It has a bushy, long tail like a cart.
It has long, floppy ears like a blanket in the wind.
It has a fluffy mane like a lion.
It has clicking hooves like a horse.
It has a stripy back like a giant panda.
It has a black and white bottom like a black, fluffy dog.
What is it?

Answer: A zebra.

Jack Birtwistle (7)
Marsh Green Primary School, Marsh Green

What Am I?

It has big, strong legs like a tree stump.
It has a muscular body like a sumo wrestler.
It has a wonky grey trunk like a worm.
It has smooth skin like rubber.
It has mysterious eyes like an owl.
It has a serious face like a lion.
It has a curly trunk like an acrobat doing a somersault.
It has curly white tusks like snow.
It has a big body like a house.
What is it?

Answer: An elegant elephant.

Ruby-Jean Foster-Finlay (7)
Marsh Green Primary School, Marsh Green

What Is It?

It has strong arms like the trees.
It has a big head like a statue's head.
It has a big body like a hard rock.
It has smelly breath like a rubbish truck.
It has a fluffy back like a fluffy rug.
It has a big belly like a bowling ball.
It has big hands like a big glove.
It has a flat nose like a pancake.
What is it?

Answer: A gorilla.

Leon Hogan (6)
Marsh Green Primary School, Marsh Green

The Secret Stomper!

It has a long, skinny tail like a stick in the wind.
It has black, beady eyes like a black circle.
It has big floppy ears like a yoga mat.
It has thick, strong legs like a thick bottle.
It has black, dark hooves like a dark door.
It has a grey-coloured body like a balloon.
What is it?

Answer: An elephant.

Grace Rollins (7)
Marsh Green Primary School, Marsh Green

The Zoo Safari

It has little ears like a zebra.
It has a black mouth like a dog.
It has sharp nails like a cat.
It has a skinny tail like a stick.
It has little ears like a baby.
It has a long neck like a tall tree.
It has long legs like a tall human.
What is it?

Answer: A giraffe.

Ava-Mae Rollins (7)
Marsh Green Primary School, Marsh Green

What Is It?

It has gigantic, huge ears like a flag in the wind.
It has a long trunk like a long stick.
It is grey like concrete.
It has long tusks like a long list.
It has small, beady eyes like a giraffe.
It is huge and it is good at listening.
What is it?

Answer: An elephant.

Julia Lubowiecka (7)
Marsh Green Primary School, Marsh Green

The Stinky Zoo

Strong beak like a rock-solid stone.
Green feathers like grass.
Black, beady eyes like a spider.
It has colourful feathers like a pen.
Pitch-black beak like a pitch-black spoon.
Blue and pink feathers like a piece of
bubblegum.
What is it?

Answer: A parrot.

Logan Davidson (7)
Marsh Green Primary School, Marsh Green

What Am I?

I am as elegant as a ballerina.
I am as intelligent as a person.
I have strong, muscular legs like a
bodybuilder.
I am mostly quiet like a slipper.
I am gentle like the summer breeze.
My spots are different like fingerprints.
What am I?

Answer: A giraffe.

Lily Hoang (6)
Marsh Green Primary School, Marsh Green

The Hard Tusks

It has sharp white tusks like a fork.
It has a long, curly trunk like wavy hair.
It has small beady eyes like black buttons.
It has long, floppy ears like a blanket in the wind.
It has sharp, pointy nails like a dog.
What is it?

Answer: An elephant.

Sienna Pennington (7)
Marsh Green Primary School, Marsh Green

What Am I?

My tusks are sharp like a knife.
My skin is wrinkly like a raisin.
My ears are flappy like a bird's wings.
My feet are as big as a mountain.
I am as loud as a trumpet.
I am grey like a stormy day.
What am I?

Answer: An elephant.

Kasey Leyland (7), Libby, Sofia Popovici (7), Lewis Adams (7) & Ella-Mae Browitt (7)

Marsh Green Primary School, Marsh Green

Unique Zoo

It has a wet nose like a dog.
It has eyes like an elephant.
It has strong legs like a horse.
It has pointy ears like a bunny.
It has big, frizzy hair like a mohawk.
It has a big bottom like an elephant.
What is it?

Answer: A zebra.

Keira O'Connell (7)
Marsh Green Primary School, Marsh Green

What Am I?

I have hands like a human.
My tail is curly like a caterpillar.
I can camouflage myself.
I am sneaky like a robber.
I can be as colourful as a rainbow.
I have a long body.
What animal could I be?

Answer: A chameleon.

Anson He (5)
Marsh Green Primary School, Marsh Green

What Is It?

It is as colourful as a parrot.
It is as blue as the ocean.
It has feathers as long as a snake.
It walks as elegant as a princess.
Its feathers are as fluffy as a teddy bear.
What animal could it be?

Answer: A peacock.

Ezmai-Rose Pilling (6), Teja (5) & James Cullen (6)
Marsh Green Primary School, Marsh Green

What Is It?

It is as colourful as a parrot.
It is as blue as the ocean.
It has feathers as long as a snake.
It walks as elegant as a princess.
It has feathers as fluffy as a teddy bear.
What animal could it be?

Answer: A peacock.

Gabriella Zefelde (5)

Marsh Green Primary School, Marsh Green

What Am I?

I have strong, muscular legs like a ninja.
I am fast like a cheetah.
My legs are like skinny toothpicks.
I have a strong neck like a skyscraper.
I have a spotty body like a ladybug.
What am I?

Answer: A giraffe.

Lexi Jo Gallagher (7)
Marsh Green Primary School, Marsh Green

What Is It?

It is as sneaky as a robber.
It has hands as human as mine.
It has a tongue as stretchy as slime.
It looks scaly like a lizard.
It's as colourful as a rainbow.
What animal could it be?

Answer: A chameleon.

Scarlett Highton (6)
Marsh Green Primary School, Marsh Green

What Am I?

I am as colourful as a rainbow.
My tongue is stretchy like slime.
I am spiky like a hedgehog.
I am scaly like a lizard.
I have a green body with a curly tail.
What animal could I be?

Answer: A chameleon.

Grace Liptrot (6)
Marsh Green Primary School, Marsh Green

The Zoo Safari

It has long wings like a bird.
It has a small head like a baby.
It has soft feathers like a bird.
It has a pointy beak like a goose.
It has small eyes like a baby's.
What is it?

Answer: A parrot.

Evie-Mai Sedgwick (6)
Marsh Green Primary School, Marsh Green

74

What Am I?

My tusks are sharp like a knife.
My ears are flappy like a bird's wings.
My feet are as big as a mountain.
I am as loud as a trumpet.
I am grey like a stormy day.
What am I?

Answer: An elephant.

Samuel Mikolajow (7)
Marsh Green Primary School, Marsh Green

What Am I?

It changes its skin colour.
It is as long as a snake.
It is as sneaky as a mouse.
It is as colourful as a rainbow.
It has hands as human as mine.
What could my animal be?

Answer: A chameleon.

Jake Ademola (5)
Marsh Green Primary School, Marsh Green

What Am I?

I am as fast as a jumbo jet.
I am stripy like a candy cane.
I am as graceful as a ballerina.
I am black and white like a humbug.
My tail is as thin as a pencil.
What am I?

Answer: A zebra.

Lola Cottom (7)
Marsh Green Primary School, Marsh Green

What Am I?

I am as fast as a jumbo jet.
I am stripy like a candy cane.
I am graceful like a ballerina.
I am black and white like a humbug.
My tail is as thin as a pencil.
What am I?

Answer: A zebra.

Alfie Wilson (7)
Marsh Green Primary School, Marsh Green

What Am I?

I am as fast as a jumbo jet.
I am stripy like a candy cane.
I am graceful like a ballerina.
I am black and white like a humbug.
My tail is thin like a pencil.
What am I?

Answer: A zebra.

Adam Koufa (7) & Lacey

Marsh Green Primary School, Marsh Green

What Am I?

I am as tall as a tree.
I am as strong as a brick.
My skin is as gentle as the summer breeze.
I am as gentle as a flower.
My legs are as strong as a rock.
What am I?

Answer: A giraffe.

Patricia Zalitie (7)
Marsh Green Primary School, Marsh Green

What Am I?

I am gentle like a ballerina.
I am spotty like a ladybug.
My neck is as long as the River Nile.
I am slow like a turtle.
My skin is yellow like a banana.
What am I?

Answer: A giraffe.

Eki Osasuwen (7)
Marsh Green Primary School, Marsh Green

What Am I?

I am gentle like a feather.
My legs are long like the River Nile.
I am as slow as a worm.
My neck is as tall as a skyscraper.
My head is like a spike.
What am I?

Answer: A giraffe.

Wahaj Asim (7)
Marsh Green Primary School, Marsh Green

What Is It?

It has hands like a human.
It is as spiky as a hedgehog.
It has a tongue as stretchy as slime.
It has eyes that are round like a circle.
What animal could it be?

Answer: A chameleon.

Ziyad Younis (5)
Marsh Green Primary School, Marsh Green

What Is It?

It is spiky like a hedgehog.
It is as sneaky as a robber.
It has eyes as round as circles.
It is as quiet as a mouse.
What animal could it be?

Answer: A chameleon.

Leo Bradley (6)
Marsh Green Primary School, Marsh Green

What Is It?

It is green like a frog.
It is slimy like a snail.
It eats small, creepy insects.
It is as sneaky as a robber.
What animal could it be?

Answer: A chameleon.

James Hughes (6)
Marsh Green Primary School, Marsh Green

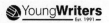

What Am I?

I am as fast as a jumbo jet.
I am stripy like a candy cane.
I am black and white like a humbug.
My tail is as thin as a pencil.
What am I?

Answer: A zebra.

Khloe O'Neil (7)
Marsh Green Primary School, Marsh Green

What Am I?

I am a mammal.
I am scared.
I am magic.
I am meek.
I eat meat.
I live at home with you.
I am the best pet.
I give a lot of love.
I am a sheemba!

Victoria Hardman (6)
Marsh Green Primary School, Marsh Green

What Am I?

I am soft like a blanket.
I swing through the trees like an acrobat.
I am cheeky!
What am I?

Answer: A monkey.

Alex Kudinov (6) & Charlie
Marsh Green Primary School, Marsh Green

What Am I?

I am a mammal.
I am weak, magical and nice.
I eat magical cake.
I live in magical clouds.
I am the best pet in the world.
I am a unicorn!

Ellie Allison (6)
Marsh Green Primary School, Marsh Green

What Am I?

I am soft like a blanket.
I swing through the trees like a swing.
I am cheeky!
What am I?

Answer: A monkey.

Paul Doherty (7)
Marsh Green Primary School, Marsh Green

What Am I?

I am a mammal.
I am spotty.
I am orange.
I am terrifying.
I am nice.
I live in your house.
I hug.
I am a unicorn bunny!

Declan Charnock (5)
Marsh Green Primary School, Marsh Green

Preston-Lee's Zoo

It has black, long ears like a black dog.
It has strong, black legs like a black dog.
It has black, shiny hooves like a horse.
What is it?

Preston-Lee Dover (6)
Marsh Green Primary School, Marsh Green

What Am I?

I am fluffy.
I am fierce.
I am big.
I have a mane.
I eat other animals.
I live in the zoo.
I roar.
I am a lion!

Charlie-Joe Towert (6)
Marsh Green Primary School, Marsh Green

What Am I?

I am a mammal.
I am multicoloured.
I am nice.
I am big.
I eat biscuits.
I live in a house.
I purr.
I am a cat!

Jasmine Busby (6)
Marsh Green Primary School, Marsh Green

What Am I?

I am a mammal.
I am spotty.
I am meek.
I am tiny.
I eat seeds.
I live in a cage.
I am lovely.
I am a hamster!

Annie Wheatcroft (6)
Marsh Green Primary School, Marsh Green

What Am I?

I am a mammal.
I am evil.
I am nice.
I am small.
I eat fish.
I live in a magical cloud.
I am an angel demon cat!

Nicola Jubass (6)

Marsh Green Primary School, Marsh Green

What Am I?

I am a mammal.
I am big.
I am tall.
I am cute.
I eat plants.
I live in a zoo.
I can jump.
I am a giraffe.

Emily Caine (6)
Marsh Green Primary School, Marsh Green

What Am I?

I am a fish.
I am a swimmer.
I am scary.
I am a carnivore.
I eat fish.
I live in the ocean.
I am a shark!

Oliwier Szymanski (6)
Marsh Green Primary School, Marsh Green

What Am I?

I am a fish.
I am a swimmer.
I am orange.
I am small.
I eat seaweed.
I live in the sea.
I am a goldfish!

Amelia Wojtaluk (6)
Marsh Green Primary School, Marsh Green

What Mammal Am I?

I am fluffy.
I am brown.
I am bumpy.
I eat grass.
I live in a field.
I walk.
I run.
I am a llama.

Kristian Longshaw (6)
Marsh Green Primary School, Marsh Green

What Am I?

I am a mammal.
I am cute.
I am colourful.
I eat dog food.
I like to bark.
I like to jump.
I am a dog!

Aiden Yates (6)
Marsh Green Primary School, Marsh Green

What Am I?

I am a fish.
I am meek.
I am orange.
I am big.
I eat seaweed.
I live in the sea.
I am a goldfish!

Kaitlin Musgrove (5)
Marsh Green Primary School, Marsh Green

What Am I?

I am a mammal.
I am magical.
I am fast.
I eat magical cake.
I live in magical clouds.
I am a unicorn.

Jack Walker (6)
Marsh Green Primary School, Marsh Green

What Am I?

I am a reptile.
I am massive.
I am bad.
I am mean.
I eat other animals.
I am a T-rex.

Leo Peet (6)
Marsh Green Primary School, Marsh Green

Animal Poem

It has orange skin.
It is not like any other animal.
It has black stripes.
It eats its prey because it is a wild animal.
It runs like electricity because it is fast.
It is a carnivore because it eats meat.
It lives in the wild jungle.
It pounces on its prey because it's wild.
It searches for its prey because it is wild.
It smells its prey.
What is it?

Answer: A tiger.

Jayden Bamfo (7)
Saint Pierre School, Leigh-On-Sea

YoungWriters Est. 1991

What Is It?

Slithery, sneaky and scaly.
It's hungry for fresh eggs from a nest.
Slithering all day long.
In its sharp fangs, it has venom for
protection.
It lives in trees or in a hole underground.
It slithers all day, looking for lunch.
It's smooth and scaly.
It swallows people whole, in one gulp.
It rattles its tail in the burning hot desert.
What is it?

Answer: A rattlesnake.

Cornelius Oberholzer (7)
Saint Pierre School, Leigh-On-Sea

What Is It?

Dark and cruel when freezing.
Goes behind the grass and pounces on its prey.
Ears can hear like humans, just better.
Lives in the African plains.
Perfect skills to chase its prey.
Whiskers blow like the wind, *whoosh!*
Furious when fighting its enemy.
Turbo fast like a brand-new turbo cat.
It is a very wild animal.
What is it?

Answer: A cheetah.

Keidi Okpue (7)
Saint Pierre School, Leigh-On-Sea

Animal Safari

It lives on a farm and it eats grass.
It plays with water.
It jumps a little.
It has a little bit of brown on it.
They like to have fun with one another.
They like to run a little but they walk fast.
It sleeps in a comfy, soft place.
It has a white body.
Its eyes are green and blue.
It is like a polar bear.
What is it?

Answer: A lamb.

Holly Rye (7)
Saint Pierre School, Leigh-On-Sea

Guess Me

I move my eyes separately.
I have a long, sticky tongue to catch my
food - flies.
I am different colours like the rainbow.
I crawl like a baby around Asia or the
tropical jungle.
Even my eyes are different colours.
I change colour when I'm on something to
camouflage from any predators.
What am I?

Answer: A chameleon.

Phoebe Norris (7)
Saint Pierre School, Leigh-On-Sea

Safari Animal

Orange or gold fur and a dark orange mane to blend in with the hot, reflecting sun.
Very sharp, white, dangerous teeth to kill its prey.
Has to sneak very low and moves slowly, then jumps high.
Humans have to be really careful of this animal that lives in the plains.
What is it?

Answer: A lion.

Pendo Mbugua (6)
Saint Pierre School, Leigh-On-Sea

Unicorns

U nder the moon, the unicorn was dancing

N ight-time came and the unicorns came out

I love unicorns!

C olourful unicorns dancing around

O utside, the unicorns were dancing

R oses came out when they danced on the grass

N ovember the 15th, they had a party!

Esmé Bragard (6)
Saint Pierre School, Leigh-On-Sea

My Best Pet

Its ears are floppy and wiggly like jelly.
Its tail wiggles when it is excited.
It sleeps on a comfy, soft pillow.
It runs as quick as lightning.
Its nose is a black as space.
Its fur is as brown as fudge.
It lives in a home.
What is it?

Answer: A dog.

Molly Dumpleton (7)
Saint Pierre School, Leigh-On-Sea

What Is It?

Claws to hunt for the luxurious meat.
Running through the African dirt.
Furry, pitch-black skin like the night sky.
Pounces to attack its prey.
Ears like knives.
It's as fast as a Mercedes-AMG GT.
What is it?

Answer: A panther.

Monty Millson (7)
Saint Pierre School, Leigh-On-Sea

Guess My Animal

It is warm, snuggly and fluffy.
It climbs trees slowly with its sharp claws.
It has big ears and they wiggle about.
It slowly walks on the ground like a bear but it is not a bear.
It is grey and fluffy.
What is it?

Answer: A koala.

Ethan-Sanders Tafadzwa Kanyepi (7)
Saint Pierre School, Leigh-On-Sea

Dragons

D ragons are nasty!
R ound people, the dragons breathe fire
A bove the clouds, dragons fly
G lowing fire from the dragon's mouth
O ctober, dragons huddle
N ear people, dragons breathe fire.

Henry Brown (5)
Saint Pierre School, Leigh-On-Sea

Rabbit

R abbits eat carrots and oranges,
A nd they are soft and white,
B aby rabbits are scared,
B eautiful rabbits are the best,
I have got a pet rabbit,
T he rabbits are silly.

Bella Hemmings (6)
Saint Pierre School, Leigh-On-Sea

Guess The Animal

Its eyes are like dots.
It eats meat and it has soft ears.
It runs really fast.
It has soft fur and is cuddly.
It has sharp teeth.
Its claws are sharp.
Its tail is big.
What is it?

Marley Wilson (7)
Saint Pierre School, Leigh-On-Sea

Guess The Creature

My antennae look like straw
And if you hold me, you will get hurt.
I have a furry tummy
And I live in the plains.
I'm orange like fire,
You can't even see my eyes.
What am I?

Sara Khan (6)
Saint Pierre School, Leigh-On-Sea

Turtles

T urtles have bumpy shells
U nder the sea, they swim around
R eally speedy
T urtles lay eggs on the sand
L arge patterned shells
E ating lots of coral.

Emmeline Longhurst (6)
Saint Pierre School, Leigh-On-Sea

Tigers

T igers like to sleep in the day
I n the night, they hunt
G oats are prey to tigers
E very day, tigers hunt something down
R are types of tigers are white tigers.

Rory Wainwright (6)
Saint Pierre School, Leigh-On-Sea

Rabbit

R abbits like eating carrots
A rabbit is hopping
B aby rabbits are cute
B aby rabbits play outside
I 've got a rabbit
T he rabbit was running.

Jorey Kyei-Bamfo (5)
Saint Pierre School, Leigh-On-Sea

Snake

S nakes in the jungle
N o snakes are allowed!
A bout snakes... They're good!
K eep snakes in your room
E ggs are healthy for snakes.

Leo Jarvis (6)

Saint Pierre School, Leigh-On-Sea

Lynx

L ittle Lynx is always happy
Y ou should look after lynxes
N ever take a lynx home as a pet
X -rays show a lynx's bones.

Nelly Cottage (6)
Saint Pierre School, Leigh-On-Sea

Snake

S nakes are scary
N ever touch snakes
A snake is dangerous
K eep away from snakes
E very snake is dangerous!

Theodore Hoad (6)

Saint Pierre School, Leigh-On-Sea

Horse

H orses eat hay
O r apples
R iding horses is fun!
S he is well behaved
E very day!

Sabrina Dearson (6)
Saint Pierre School, Leigh-On-Sea

Tigers

Tigers smell damp and cold like birds, and like raw meat with bones in the night.
Tigers feel like a nice, soft bunny rabbit but believe me - you wouldn't touch one or you'd turn from a human into dinner!
Tigers sound like a raging beast roaring with might like a thunderbolt echoing from the Earth.
Tigers taste like a fluffy ball and the blood of their prey.
Tigers look like a fire with black and orange stripes and a little bit of white.

Frank Garvey (6)
St Joseph's Catholic Primary School, Upminster

Stitch

Stitch tastes like bones, dog treats and water.
Stitch smells like a bubble bath or horse poo... Yuck!
Stitch looks like a furball lying on the bed.
Stitch sounds like a crying whale when he loses his toy.
When he eats, he goes *crunch, crunch, crunch!*
Stitch feels soft and fluffy like my favourite toy.
I love Stitch, he's the one I love the most.

Millie Lavey (7)
St Joseph's Catholic Primary School, Upminster

Horse Sense Poem

Horses look brown, white and black like the night sky.
Horses feel smooth but their mane is dirty and tangled from galloping in the wind.
Horses smell like hay, apples, carrots and mud after jumping in puddles of water.
Horses sound noisy when they go *neigh, snort!* They whine if they want you to ride on them.
Horses taste like fresh water and green grass.

Maria Rasskazova (7)
St Joseph's Catholic Primary School, Upminster

Penguin Sense Poem

Penguins taste like salty fish, all cold and rotten. *Ewww!*
Penguins smell like the deep blue sea.
Penguins feel soft like a blanket but their legs are really rough.
Penguins sound like *squawk, splash, peck!* They're too noisy!
Penguins have a dark back that's as black as the night and a bright white tummy like the moonlight.

Darcy Davies (7)
St Joseph's Catholic Primary School, Upminster

Chihuahua Sense Poem

Chihuahuas look like a small fluffball covered in moss.
Chihuahuas smell like fresh grass.
Chihuahuas sound like a loud *woof*, *pant* and *yap!* What a lot of noise!
Chihuahuas feel like a soft pillow on a comfy bed.
Chihuahuas taste like dog food and dinosaur bones buried in the ground.

Molly Tobin (6)

St Joseph's Catholic Primary School, Upminster

Giraffe Sense Poem

Giraffes smell as smelly as melted chocolate.
Giraffes would look beautiful even with golden eyes, short necks, big bodies and pink stripes.
Giraffes sound as loud as a *raaaa!*
Giraffes feel as rough and bumpy as a rock that is solid and hard.
Giraffes taste as spicy as a burning hot chilli.

Penny Restarick (7)

St Joseph's Catholic Primary School, Upminster

My Cat Sense Poem

My cat looks like a chubby, fluffy hairball.
My cat sounds like *miaow, purr, hiss!*
My cat feels soft, warm and cuddly like a
fluffy cloud.
My cat smells like rotten mice, milk and
tuna (his favourite midnight feast!).
My cat tastes like fresh milk and salmon
after breakfast.

Patrick Fuller (7)
St Joseph's Catholic Primary School, Upminster

Kangaroo Sense Poem

Kangaroos smell like beautiful, rainbow-coloured flowers.
Kangaroos look as colourful as multicoloured caterpillars.
Kangaroos sound like frogs jumping everywhere.
Kangaroos feel like soft pillows everywhere on a smooth cloud.
Kangaroos taste like salty crisps and crunchy sweets.

Anastazja Strzelczyk (7)
St Joseph's Catholic Primary School, Upminster

Cheetah Sense Poem

Cheetahs look like big, fluffy, yellow rugby balls covered in grass.
Cheetahs smell like meat and steak.
Cheetahs sound like roaring cats and are as loud as a dinosaur.
Cheetahs feel as soft as a cloud floating in the sky.
Cheetahs taste like rotten meat and steak.

Somto Iwu (6)

St Joseph's Catholic Primary School, Upminster

Horse Sense Poem

Horses taste like a sweet chocolate muffin
with flies on it. Disgusting!
Horses smell like hay and a farmyard full of
animals.
Horses have very fast eyesight.
Horses sound like *neigh, clip-clop* and *swish!*
Horses feel like a soft, warm teddy bear.

Hugo Willis (7)
St Joseph's Catholic Primary School, Upminster

My Budgie Mango

Mango looks like a feathery ball as blue as the sky.

Mango smells like fresh air.

Mango sounds noisy with a *squawk, cheep, chirp!*

Mango feels all fluffy like a warm blanket.

Mango tastes all yucky with seeds on top.

I love my budgie Mango.

Olive Etherington (7)

St Joseph's Catholic Primary School, Upminster

Elephant Sense Poem

Elephants look grey, have big ears and big stomping feet.
Elephants smell like grass, water and mud.
Elephants sound like loud trumpets and big stomping feet.
Elephants taste like meat - chewy and hard.
Elephants feel like a wrinkly, soft carpet.

Arthur Hill (7)
St Joseph's Catholic Primary School, Upminster

Gecko Sense

Geckos look like a big green ball and a scaly dragon.
Geckos smell like a dirty dumpster and rotten veg.
Geckos sound squeaky like a scratchy monster.
Geckos feel rough like a scaly alligator.
Geckos taste like juicy flies and bugs.

Grey Harding (7)
St Joseph's Catholic Primary School, Upminster

My Dog Winston

My dog looks like golden sand.
He smells like roses and dandelions.
He woofs and scratches at the door when
he wants to go into a room.
He is soft like a blanket.
My dog tastes like ham and sausages.
I love Winston.

Kitty Tyler (6)
St Joseph's Catholic Primary School, Upminster

Tiger Sense Poem

My tiger smells like marshmallows and wafers.
My tiger looks like rainbows with purple eyes.
My tiger sounds like music instead of growling.
My tiger feels like fluffy cotton candy.
My tiger tastes like amazing apples.

Elsie Hosler (6)
St Joseph's Catholic Primary School, Upminster

Giraffe Sensory Poem

Giraffes smell like a delicious chocolate cake.

Giraffes look handsome in hats.

Giraffes sound like a magnificent trumpet band.

Giraffes feel as soft as a teddy bear.

Giraffes taste like smelly, crumbly cheese.

Oliver Holmes (8)
St Joseph's Catholic Primary School, Upminster

Toucan Sense Poem

Toucans smell like calm and tall trees.
Toucans look like one very colourful animal.
Toucans sound like a loud bird squawking.
Toucans feel like a soft and fluffy teddy.
Toucans taste like burgers and pizza.

Lily Garrett (6)
St Joseph's Catholic Primary School, Upminster

Zebra Sense Poem

Zebras smell like a rainbow marshmallow.
Zebras look like a magical forest.
Zebras sound like puffing and a piano sound.
Zebras feel like a soft feather.
Zebras taste like magical rainbow chocolate.

Sophia Jackson (7)
St Joseph's Catholic Primary School, Upminster

Giraffe Sense Poem

Giraffes smell like the beach on the hottest day of the year.
Giraffes look very spotty like a Dalmatian.
Giraffes sound like a bear.
Giraffes feel like a fluffy pillow.
Giraffes taste like a bird.

Alice Fletcher (6)

St Joseph's Catholic Primary School, Upminster

Lion Sense Poem

Lions smell like wild wind and wet grass.
Lions look like a flaming fire.
Lions feel furry and soft but you don't want to stroke them.
Lions taste like meat and the blood of their prey.

Nico Vannoli Rogacz (7)

St Joseph's Catholic Primary School, Upminster

Peacock Sense Poem

Peacocks smell like a fresh breeze.
Peacocks look like fashionistas.
Peacocks sound like a bird's whistle.
Peacocks feel as delicate as a feather.
Peacocks taste like pepper.

Elizabeth Mahoney (7)
St Joseph's Catholic Primary School, Upminster

Elephant Sense Poem

Elephants smell like freshwater.
Elephants look very colourful.
Elephants sound like they're whistling.
Elephants feel furry and cuddly.
Elephants taste like sour gummies.

Ryan Arun (7)
St Joseph's Catholic Primary School, Upminster

Cat Sense Poem

A cat looks like a warm teddy.
A cat smells like fish and the ocean.
A cat sounds like a hiss and a miaow!
A cat feels like a soft cushion.
A cat tastes like a hairball.

Millie Allen (6)
St Joseph's Catholic Primary School, Upminster

Only The Lonely Shark

Only the shark swam all day,
No fish would come and play.
He looked too scary for them to meet;
Only could have the fish to eat.
The starfish was not scared of him,
She wanted to play on his fin!
Now Only was not lonely anymore
And the two swam from shore to shore.
The story of Only and the starfish was told far and wide,
As they swam and leapt with the tide;
They showed that just because someone is different to you,
Doesn't mean they can't be your best friend too!

Jago Sandilands (6)
St Joseph's Catholic School, Malmesbury

My Flamingo

My flamingo lives in South Africa.
My flamingo eats pink shrimps.
My flamingo stands on one leg.
My flamingo bends over to drink the water.
My flamingo is pink with fluffy feathers.
My flamingo flies to her nest.

Lara (5)

St Joseph's Catholic School, Malmesbury

The Lion

King of the jungle.
A giant cat! Very soft!
Eats meat in the sun.
Living wild in Africa.
Hunting and roaring all day.
The lion is fierce!
The lion is brave!
King of the jungle.

Finn Stannard (5)
St Joseph's Catholic School, Malmesbury

My Koala

My koala is grey and fluffy.
My koala has four thumbs.
My koala has big ears.
My koala eats eucalyptus leaves.
My koala lives in the trees in Australia.
My koala sleeps all day.

Jaz (5)
St Joseph's Catholic School, Malmesbury

The Happy Bunny

Silly bunny, very fluffy.
Carrots, radishes and lettuce,
Yummy, yummy in my tummy,
Running, jumping, playing.
Somersaulting in the sun,
Being a bunny is so much fun!

Florence Gray (5)
St Joseph's Catholic School, Malmesbury

Hungry Spider

My tarantula is big and hairy,
I gave him a name so he wasn't scary.
I took him into the garden,
to look at the sky,
and when he was hungry,
he ate a fly.

Josh Davison (6)
St Joseph's Catholic School, Malmesbury

Happy Rabbit

His eyes are beautiful, his tail is soft
And he always likes to be cheerful.
He jumps high and is everywhere,
May the rabbit always be happy.

Victoria Mroszczyk (5)
St Joseph's Catholic School, Malmesbury

Monkey Time

Once there was a monkey called Milly,
She played with her friends and was silly.
She swung in the trees,
Her mummy picked her fleas.

Rosalie Andreou (5)
St Joseph's Catholic School, Malmesbury

Silly Monkey

My monkey is very silly,
He is very playful too.
He might jump on your car,
Because he wants to play with you.

Ottilie Beswick (5)

St Joseph's Catholic School, Malmesbury

Licky The Lizard

Licky the lizard is green,
He likes to lick cream.
He lives in the forest,
With his mate Boris.

Caleb Chapman (4)
St Joseph's Catholic School, Malmesbury

Flash Fred The Shark

My shark's name is Fred
And he lives on Mars.
He sleeps in bed
And has fast cars.

Thomas Pilkington (5)
St Joseph's Catholic School, Malmesbury

My Unicorn Poem

Unicorns smell like sweet cupcakes and sweet things.
Unicorns look like fancy, mysterious, rare creatures.
Unicorns sound like horses laughing at a party but a bit quieter.
Unicorns feel super soft with beautiful multicoloured skin.
Unicorns taste like glittery doughnuts and cupcakes.
Unicorn power!

Olivia Connor (7)
St Vincent's Catholic Primary School, Penketh

My Rabbit Poem

Rabbits smell like muddy, squelchy hay,
especially on a rainy day.
A rabbit looks like a furry, bouncy
cannonball, some are big and some are
small.
Rabbits sound like little hamsters squeaking
and are very cute when they are sleeping.
Rabbits feel like the softest silk.
I love rabbits.

Clemency Ryan-Stout (7)
St Vincent's Catholic Primary School, Penketh

My Pet Dog

Bobby smells like little fish and raw meat.
Bobby looks cute and tiny but he's actually
very cheeky!
Bobby sounds like a bunch of crying babies
when he cries.
Bobby feels very warm and cuddly like his
soft bed.
Bobby tastes like fish and doggy ice cream.
And... I love Bobby!

Lottie Corbett (7)

St Vincent's Catholic Primary School, Penketh

Cheetahs

Cheetahs smell like a black and orange banana, all ripe and sweet.
Cheetahs eat meat, all fresh and sweet.
Cheetahs look all calm and cute but they are fearsome and angry.
Cheetahs sound like a group of teenagers bunched together, screaming.
Cheetahs feel very fluffy like my bed.

William Chaplin (7)
St Vincent's Catholic Primary School, Penketh

My Dogs Sense Poem

Dogs smell like dog treats and dog bones with sweat on them.
Dogs look like a soft and fluffy blanket.
Dogs sound like people shouting at a party.
Dogs feel like a fluffy, warm pillow.
Dogs taste like dog treats with hair on them!
I love dogs!

Daisy-Mai Winsor (7)
St Vincent's Catholic Primary School, Penketh

My Unicorn Sense Poem

Unicorns smell like cupcakes and jam doughnuts!
Unicorns look cute, fluffy and colourful just like my favourite bear.
Unicorns sound like a quiet horse clip-clopping in a field.
Unicorns taste like hairy cupcakes.
I love unicorns!

Elise Vernon (7)

St Vincent's Catholic Primary School, Penketh

My Pet Figaro

My pet Figaro smells sweet like a cupcake.
My pet Figaro looks cute and cuddly like a pillow.
My pet Figaro sounds like lots of mice squeaking.
My pet Figaro feels soft and fluffy.
My pet Figaro tastes like meat with hair on it!

Macy Winn (7)
St Vincent's Catholic Primary School, Penketh

My Pig Sense Poem

Pigs smell like brown, dirty dust.
Pigs taste like bacon and ham!
Pigs feel wrinkly and a bit hairy.
Pigs look like little, cute, pink rascals.
Pigs sound like fireworks banging out loud!
I love pigs!

Lottie Dean (7)

St Vincent's Catholic Primary School, Penketh

My Horse Poem

Horses smell like dirty hay.
Horses look like a stuffed teddy.
Horses sound like a clapping person.
Horses feel like a soft blanket.
Horses taste like some soggy hay and
apples.
I love horses!

Isabelle Hodgkin (7)
St Vincent's Catholic Primary School, Penketh

My Dogs

Dogs smell like mints.
Dogs look like cute teddies.
Dogs sound like loud fireworks.
Dogs feel like soft, fluffy bunnies.
Dogs taste like sweet chocolate.
I love dogs.

Aimee Moss (7)
St Vincent's Catholic Primary School, Penketh

What Am I?

I am extremely big.
I am grey.
I have a curly tail.
I have round feet.
I am nearly extinct.
I eat juicy grass.
I can be brown.
I am an elephant!

Rageh Biviji (6)
St Vincent's Catholic Primary School, Penketh

What Is It?

It has a long neck.
It eats leaves from the trees.
It walks slowly.
It has hooves.
It has little horns.
It is yellow and brown.
It is a giraffe!

Harris Weston (6)

St Vincent's Catholic Primary School, Penketh

What Am I?

I am a carnivore.
I like to eat meat.
I live in the South Pole.
I have layers of fat under my skin.
I like swimming deep underwater.
I am a penguin!

Mia Hughes (6)
St Vincent's Catholic Primary School, Penketh

What Is It?

It is super fast.
It hunts for its prey.
It has sharp claws.
It has four paws.
It lives in the wild.
It is extremely scary.
It is a cheetah!

Joel Gawne-Sheridan (6)
St Vincent's Catholic Primary School, Penketh

Molly

Molly smells like meat.
Molly looks black and white.
Molly sounds like loud thunder.
Molly feels like furry hamsters.
Molly tastes like meat and fur.

Frankie Lloyd (7)
St Vincent's Catholic Primary School, Penketh

What Am I?

I have soft fur.
I have pointy ears.
I have four paws.
I love to eat mice.
I am very quiet.
I have an owner.
I am a cat!

Jessica Croughan (5)
St Vincent's Catholic Primary School, Penketh

What Am I?

I am a carnivore.
I have sharp teeth.
I hunt for animals.
I am fierce.
I have orange eyes.
I am a sabre-toothed tiger!

Libby Thompson (6)
St Vincent's Catholic Primary School, Penketh

What Am I?

I am very cute.
I have sharp claws.
I have three fingers.
I live in Chester Zoo.
I am slow.
I am a sloth!

Thea Halsall (5)

St Vincent's Catholic Primary School, Penketh

What Is It?

It has a mane.
It is yellow.
It has sharp paws.
It has sharp teeth.
It is super fast.
It is a lion!

Shannon Albinson (6)
St Vincent's Catholic Primary School, Penketh

What Am I?

I am super fast.
I am spotty.
I am orange.
I live in the wild.
I have a tail.
I am a cheetah!

Maddie Lockwood (6)
St Vincent's Catholic Primary School, Penketh

Tom And Jerry

I am grey.
I chase Jerry the mouse.
I don't like cheese.
I live in a house.
I am Tom the cat!

Daniel Moore (5)
St Vincent's Catholic Primary School, Penketh

What Am I?

I am scary.
I am terrifying and orange.
I scare people.
I run very fast.
I am a cheetah!

Oliver Graham (5)
St Vincent's Catholic Primary School, Penketh

What Am I?

I am orange.
I have black spots.
I have whiskers.
I am scary.
I am a leopard!

Bonnie Fagan (6)
St Vincent's Catholic Primary School, Penketh

What Is It?

It is fast.
It is rainbow coloured.
It lives in a zoo.
It is a cheetah!

Ivy Harrison (5)
St Vincent's Catholic Primary School, Penketh

YOUNG WRITERS INFORMATION

We hope you have enjoyed reading this book – and that you will continue to in the coming years.

If you're the parent or family member of an enthusiastic poet or story writer, do visit our website **www.youngwriters.co.uk/subscribe** and sign up to receive news, competitions, writing challenges and tips, activities and much, much more! There's lots to keep budding writers motivated!

If you would like to order further copies of this book, or any of our other titles, then please give us a call or order via your online account.

Young Writers
Remus House
Coltsfoot Drive
Peterborough
PE2 9BF
(01733) 890066
info@youngwriters.co.uk

Join in the conversation!
Tips, news, giveaways and much more!

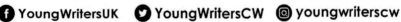 YoungWritersUK YoungWritersCW youngwriterscw